# A NATION CRUMBLES

**TRUTH PUBLICATIONS, INC.**
**CEI BOOKSTORE**
PO Box 1056, Athens, AL 35612
www.truthbooks.com

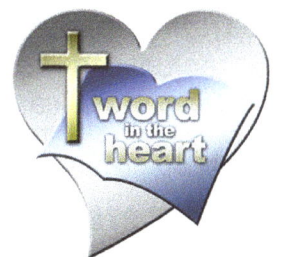

word in the heart

6:2

# A Nation Crumbles

## Table of Contents

**Cover Photo:** When Jeroboam became king, he built altars at Dan and Bethel so the people would not return to Jerusalem to worship. Archaeologists have uncovered the holy precinct at Dan.

ISBN 10: 1-58427-304-6

ISBN 13: 978-158427-304-2

First Printing: 2016

# The Kingdom Divided

**Lesson Objective:**
To emphasize that the nation was divided into two parts—Israel and Judah.

## MEMORY VERSE

*"But he rejected the advice which the elders had given him, and consulted the young men who had grown up with him, who stood before him" (1 Kings 12:8).*

**READ:** 1 Kings 12:1-33 (See also 2 Chron. 10:1-11:17).

**WHAT YOU WILL STUDY:** In this lesson, you will see how ten of the twelve tribes of Israel rebelled against their ruler (Rehoboam) and set up another kingdom called Israel (ruled by Jeroboam).

## The Story

Solomon, the king of Israel, had just died, and Israel needed a new king. And so, Rehoboam, Solomon's son, was made king over the twelve tribes. Solomon had built many great buildings (such as the temple), but high taxes had been necessary for this. Now, the people wanted a change. Under the leadership of Jeroboam, these people asked Rehoboam to collect less tax money from them. King Rehoboam first asked the old men of his palace what they thought he should do. They advised him to do as the people wanted and lower the taxes. Rehoboam then asked his young advisors their advice. They told him the very opposite: if anything, ask for more tax money. And so, Rehoboam took the advice of the young men, and he told the people that he would make even higher demands of them than his father had made.

Of course, the people become very angry at this. All the tribes except Judah and Benjamin rebelled against Rehoboam, and they made Jeroboam their king. Jeroboam's kingdom was called Israel, and Rehoboam's kingdom was called Judah. Rehoboam wanted to fight against the army of Israel to get back the ten tribes. God told Rehoboam not to do that, for this division of the kingdom had come to pass because God desired it. Rehoboam obeyed God and did not fight.

On the other hand, Jeroboam disobeyed God. He was afraid the people of Israel would go back to Jerusalem (which was in Judah) to worship God, would begin to like Rehoboam, and would then reject Jeroboam as their king. And so, Jeroboam built two idols—one in Dan and one in Bethel. The people then worshipped these idols instead of Jehovah.

## What You Should Learn

*1. Rehoboam lost most of his kingdom because he did not listen to the older, more experienced men.* (See Ephesians 6:4.)

*2. Jeroboam lost the favor of God because he did not worship Jehovah.* (See Matt. 4:10.)

## Review

### Short Answer

1. What favor did the people ask of Rehoboam? _____

_____

2. How many days did Rehoboam think about the request? _____

3. Who was made the king of Israel? _____

4. What was Rehoboam's kingdom called? _____

The sacred precinct which Jeroboam erected at Dan has been excavated. The metal replica of the altar gives one a perspective of what the original looked like.

5. How many men were ready to fight in Rehoboam's army? _____

6. Why didn't Rehoboam's army fight Israel?_____

   _____

7. Why did Jeroboam build idols in Israel?_____

   _____

8. What were these idols? _____

9. What were the two cities in which the idols were built? _____

   _____

10. What time of the year did Jeroboam and his people sacrifice to these idols? _____

## Matching

| | |
|---|---|
| _____ 1. He had to flee from Israel to Egypt while Solomon lived. | a. Judah |
| _____ 2. Rehoboam was appointed king in this city. | b. Shemaiah |
| _____ 3. He was the messenger of God to Jeroboam. | c. Jeroboam |
| _____ 4. He was a tax collector who was stoned to death. | d. Benjamin |
| _____ 5. He had to flee to Jerusalem from Shechem. | e. Ephraim |
| _____ 6-7. These two tribes made up Rehoboam's kingdom. | f. Ahijah the Shilonite |
| | g. Rehoboam |
| _____ 8. He was the messenger of God to Rehoboam. | h. Shechem |
| _____ 9. Jeroboam lived in this land. | i. Adoram |

## Map Study:

(You may need to check the more detailed map on page 64 for answering these questions.)

1. Locate these places:

   a. Reuben

   b. Gad

   c. Eastern Manasseh

   d. Judah

   e. Ephraim

   f. Western Manasseh

   g. Benjamin

   h. Simeon

   i. Zebulun

   j. Issachar

   k. Asher

   l. Naphtali

   m. Dan (country)

   n. Shechem

   o. Jerusalem

   p. Bethel

   q. Dan (city)

2. Draw a heavy line on the border between the kingdoms of Israel and Judah. Color the kingdom of Judah.

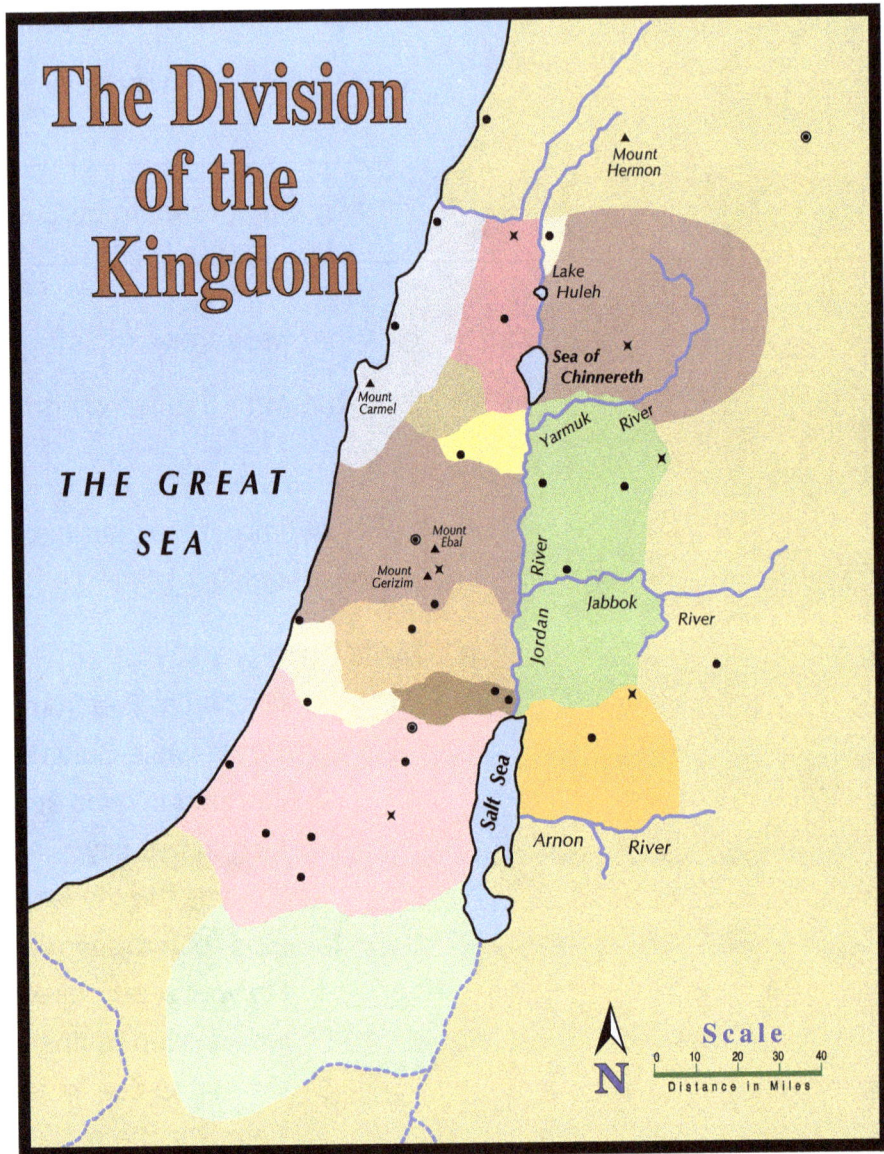

**The Division of the Kingdom**

Mount Hermon

Lake Huleh

Sea of Chinnereth

Mount Carmel

Yarmuk River

THE GREAT SEA

Mount Ebal

Mount Gerizim

Jordan River

Jabbok River

Salt Sea

Arnon River

**Scale**

0  10  20  30  40

Distance in Miles

N

*Words to Know*

"Faith"—conviction of the truth of something (Thayer, pistis)

6

# A Bad King and Queen

**READ:** 1 Kings 16:29-34; 19:1-18; 21:1-29; 22:29-38; 2 Kings 9:30-37.

**WHAT YOU WILL STUDY:** In this lesson, you will see how a prophet of God (Elijah) stood against a very wicked king and his wife (Ahab and Jezebel).

## Lesson Objective:
To show the danger that evil companions pose to one's soul.

## The Story

About thirty-five years after king Jeroboam died, Ahab became king over Israel. Very soon Ahab did things which did not please God: "And Ahab the son of Omni did evil in the sight of the Lord more than all who were before him" (1 Kings 16:30). Ahab married Jezebel, and this woman made Ahab even more wicked. Ahab and Jezebel killed many prophets of God and began to worship an idol called Baal. Because of this great sin, God did not let rain fall upon the land of Israel for three years. At the end of these three years, a great contest was held on Mt. Carmel between the prophets of God and the prophets of Baal. To show who was the true God, a contest was devised in which the God who was able to light the fire on the altar would be known as the true God. The prophets of Baal failed to produce fire, but God lit the fire on the altar at Mt. Carmel in response to Elijah's prayer. Elijah ordered that the 450 prophets of Baal be put to death. God then permitted rain to fall upon the land. When Elijah left Mt. Carmel, he ran ahead of the chariot of Ahab from Mt. Carmel to Jezreel.

When news of this reached Jezebel, she was very angry at Elijah. In fact, she threatened to kill him. Jezebel's threat scared Elijah, and he left the land. During this time, Elijah was frightened and

## MEMORY VERSE

". . . You have sold yourself to do evil in the sight of the Lord" (1 Kings 21:20).

discouraged. He had been faithful to God, and now his own life was in danger. He felt disappointed and alone. But the Lord told him that 7,000 people still lived in Israel who had remained faithful to God. This encouraged Elijah, and he arose to do the work of God.

Shortly after this, Ahab committed a sin that was very serious in the sight of God. A man named Naboth owned a vineyard that was close to the king's palace. Ahab coveted this vineyard very much, and so he offered to buy it. Naboth did not want to sell it, and so Ahab began to pout. Jezebel asked Ahab why he would not eat or drink, and Ahab told her of Naboth's vineyard. In order to get the vineyard for her husband, Jezebel ordered Naboth to be killed. Because of this great sin, both Ahab and Jezebel were sentenced to die in the same way that Naboth died. Elijah foretold that dogs would lick the blood of Ahab and would eat Jezebel's body by the wall of Jezreel (1 Kings 21:19, 23).

In a few years, Ahab was indeed killed in a battle with the king of Syria. Ahab was wounded by an arrow that found its way through the joints of his armor. He died shortly, and dogs licked up his blood that poured from his chariot. Shortly after this, Jezebel was pushed out of an upper-story window and killed. Before her body could be buried, dogs had eaten most of it. Thus, the word of the Lord came true.

## What You Should Learn

*1. The sin of idolatry is not pleasing to God.* Ahab committed this sin by worshipping Baal. Today, we commit this same sin when we put anything in our lives before God. God must always come first (Rom. 1:25; 1 Cor. 6:9-10; Rev. 21:8).

*2. The sin of evil companionship is very displeasing to God.* Ahab married a very wicked woman, and he became more wicked because of her. We must not make friends with evil people. If we do, we will become less pleasing to God (1 Cor. 15:33).

*3. The sin of covetousness is not pleasing to God.* "Covetous-ness" means to want something so much that you would do some-thing wrong to get it. Ahab committed this sin. He wanted Naboth's vineyard, but he could not get it without killing Naboth. No one should want anything so much that he would do something wrong to get it (Heb. 13:5).

## Review

### Short Answer

1. Who was the most wicked king of Israel? _____

2. Name at least three sins that Ahab did to displease God: _____

   _____

   _____

3. What was the name of Ahab's wife? _____

4. Name the prophet of God who stood alone against Ahab._____

5. What did Ahab and Jezebel do to most of the prophets of God?

   _____

6. What did God do to Israel because of Ahab's sins?_____

   _____

7. Why did Elijah leave Israel and stay in a cave near Horeb? ___

   _____

8. How many people of Israel never worshipped Baal?_____

9. Name one thing that made Elijah so great. _____

   _____

### Multiple Choice

1. Ahab wanted the _____ that belonged to Naboth.
   a. Wife
   b. Vineyard
   c. Oxen

2. Jezebel _____ Naboth in order to get his land.
   a. Begged
   b. Paid
   c. Killed

3. Because Ahab took Naboth's vineyard, God told him:
   a. The land would prosper
   b. His life would be taken away
   c. The land would burn up

4. When Ahab heard that sentence of God, he:

   a. Laughed

   b. Prayed

   c. Sorrowed

5. Ahab died when:

   a. Elijah killed him

   b. He was in battle

   c. He killed himself

6. Jezebel died when:

   a. She fell from a window

   b. She was poisoned

   c. Ahab killed her

## Matching

_____ 1. Place where Baal was worshipped     a. Omri

_____ 2. Man who Elijah appointed to be king     b. 22

_____ 3. Number of years that Ahab was king     c. Samaria

_____ 4. Number of Baal's prophets who were     d. Hazael

          killed

_____ 5. Place to which Elijah fled     e. Elisha

_____ 6. King of Judah at time that Ahab lived     f. 3

_____ 7. Man who Elijah appointed to be king     g. Jehu

          over Israel

_____ 8. Man who Elijah appointed to be next     h. 450

          prophet of God

_____ 9. Father of Ahab     i. Horeb

_____ 10. Numbers of years that Israel had no     j. Jehoshaphat

          rain

# The Assyrian Captivity

**Lesson Objective:**
To emphasize that God's longsuffering can be exhausted.

## MEMORY VERSE

*". . . Turn from your evil ways, and keep My commandments and My statutes. . ." (2 Kings 17:13).*

**READ:** 2 Kings 14:23-29; 15:27-31; 16:1-9; 17:1-23.

**WHAT YOU WILL STUDY:** In this lesson, you will learn how and why God allowed the Israelites to be captured by the Assyrians.

## The Story

Before you can know why God's people were taken into captivity, you must understand how sinful they were. For many years, Israel and its kings had rejected God. About sixty years after Ahab died, Jeroboam II was made king of Israel. The Bible says that he was a very wicked king (2 Kings 14:24). Israel worshipped idols during the forty-one years of his reign. Idolatry became so bad that God had to send His prophets (like Amos) to preach against idols. Jeroboam died, and Pekah became king of Israel. Pekah reigned for twenty years. He was also a disobedient king just like Jeroboam (2 Kings 15:28). Idolatry was practiced during this time. It was because of this sinfulness that God allowed His people to be captured by the Assyrians.

The capture of Israel was in two parts. The first part of the capture happened when Pekah was king of Israel. Pekah joined a rebellion against Assyria. In order to force Judah to participate in the rebellion, Pekah attacked Judah and her king (Ahaz). But he knew that he could not defeat Judah alone. So he asked the king of Syria (Rezin) to help him. When the armies of Israel and Syria attacked Judah, king Ahaz needed help. Rather than trusting in God, Ahaz asked the king of Assyria, Tiglath-pileser, to help. The Assyrian army agreed to fight the army of Israel. They defeated Israel, and the northern part of Israel was captured in this flight.

The second part of Israel's capture happened after Pekah died. The next and last king of Israel was Hoshea. Hoshea ruled over sourthern Israel (Samaria) for nine years. During these years, he paid tribute money to the king of Assyria, so he could still rule on the throne. Also Hoshea stayed as evil as the kings before him (2 Kings 17:13-17). The Israelites under Hoshea committed idolatry and God was getting more and more angry with these wicked people. God sent His prophets Hosea, Isaiah, and Micah, but the people did not listen. So God let Assyria conquer the southern part of Israel (Samaria) when Hoshea did two things: (1) Hoshea tried to join with Egypt against Assyria, and (2) Hoshea stopped paying tribute money to Assyria. When Assyria captured Israel, the Israelites were not allowed to live in their own land. Many of them were deported to other parts of the Assyrian empire and people from other parts of the empire were transported into Israel. In this way, God punished Israel for its sins.

## What You Should Learn

1. *God loves men, but God hates sin.* God loved the Israelites. They were descendants of Abraham. They were in the same nation as Jacob, Joseph, Moses, David, and other great men. They were God's chosen people. But all of this did not prevent God from hating their sin and punishing them. The same thing is true today. God loves you. He wants you to go to heaven. But if you do not obey God's will, He will punish you.

2. *The nation of God did not listen to the prophets.* Because Israel was so sinful, God sent different prophets to them. These prophets preached the word of God. But the people did not listen to the prophets. They did not change their wicked ways, and God destroyed them. We must be careful not to repeat this sin. When God's word tells us we are wrong, we must change. We should never get mad and refuse to listen to God's will.

## Review

### Short Answer

1. Name the three kings of Israel that you read about in this lesson. Tell which were evil and which were good.

| King | Good or Evil? |
| --- | --- |
|  |  |
|  |  |
|  |  |

2. Name four prophets whom God sent to Israel to warn them.___

   _____

3. What country captured Israel? _____

4. Which part of Israel was captured first? _____

5. What did Pekah do to cause the first part of Israel to be captured? _____

6. How many years passed until the other part of Israel was captured? _____

7. Why did Assyria let Hoshea rule over this part of Israel for this
   length of time? _____

8. Name two things Hoshea did that caused the rest of Israel to be
   captured? _____

   _____

9. What finally happened to Hoshea? _____

10. Why did God allow Israel to be captured? _____

   _____

## Yes or No?

_____ 1. Were the countries of Syria and Assyria the same?

_____ 2. Were the men Hoshea and Hosea the same?

_____ 3. Did Israel listen to God's prophets?

_____ 4. Did God hate the sin of Israel?

_____ 5. Did God let Syria capture Israel?

**Find the Mistakes.** Circle the 10 mistakes in this paragraph.
About forty years after Ahab died, Jeroboam I was made king of
Israel. He was a wicked king because he committed the sin of adul-
tery. After Jeroboam II died, Pekah then became king. He wanted to
conquer Assyria, so he asked Judah and Syria to help him. Assyria
won the battle, though. The southern part of Israel was captured in
this battle. After Pekah died, Hosea became king of Israel. He re-

fused to pay money to King Ahaz of Sryia, so Assyria killed him and captured northern Israel.

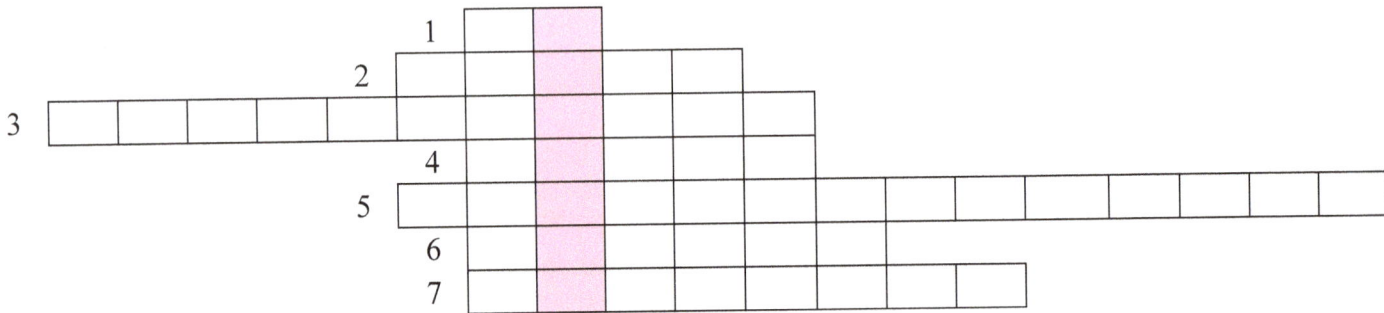

**Puzzle.** Complete the puzzle below. Use the letters in the shaded spaces to spell out a thing we should always do.

Something we should always do (shaded area):_____

**Clues:**

1. The king of Egypt that joined with Hoshea against Assyria.

2. One of the cities that the Israelites were kept in after they were captured.

3. The king of Assyria that took money from Hoshea.

4. The nation which tried to help Pekah conquer Judah.

5. The king of Assyria that conquered northern Israel.

6. The last king of Israel before the Assyrian captivity.

7. The sin Israel was guilty of.

Words to Know

**"Captivity"**—*the state of being a captive; bondage*

14

# Hezekiah

**Lesson Objective:**
To show that God hears and answers prayer.

**READ:** 2 Kings 18:1-23; 19:1-37; 20:1-21

**WHAT YOU WILL STUDY:** In this lesson, you will study a very righteous king of Judah, Hezekiah, and how he dealt with the enemy king and nation of Assyria.

## The Story

Hezekiah became king when the nation of Judah was very wicked. Hezekiah's father, king Ahaz, had built idols to worship. Hezekiah was not like his father, though. The Bible says of him: "And he did that which was right in the sight of the Lord" (2 Kings 18:3). He destroyed the idols which his father had built and trusted in the Lord. This is why the prophet of God, Isaiah, is so important in this story.

During Hezekiah's reign, his nation (Judah) had been paying tribute to the nation of Assyria. Assyria had conquered Israel, but spared Judah when Hezekiah promised to pay tribute money. The king of Assyria demanded 300 talents of silver and 30 talents of gold. In order to collect these riches, Hezekiah had to take all the king's treasury and even some of the gold from the temple. Some years after Hezekiah paid this to Assyria's king, he rebelled against Assyria and refused to pay more tribute. Sennacherib marched into Judah and defeated many cities. He then sent his messenger, Rabshakeh, to Jerusalem. Rabshakeh spoke to Eliakim, Hezekiah's messenger, and tried to persuade the government of Judah to surrender to Assyria. When Hezekiah heard of this demand for surrender, he sent word of it to Isaiah. Isaiah instructed Hezekiah not to be afraid—the Lord would cause Sennacherib to return into his own land and fight there. Jerusalem would not be conquered. The Lord was true to His promise.

Sennacherib conquered Lachish of Judah and repelled the Egyptians who were coming to assist Judah. He now was ready to march against Jerusalem. He sent a letter to Hezekiah and tried to frighten him into surrender. Hezekiah prayed to God and went to

## MEMORY VERSE

*"O Lord God of Israel, the One who dwells between the cherubim, You are God, You alone, of all the kingdoms of the earth. You have made heaven and earth" (2 Kings 19:15).*

Isaiah again. Once again, God promised that Sennacherib would not defeat Jerusalem and Judah. The Lord miraculously delivered Jerusalem by smiting to death 185,000 Assyrians. Sennacherib was forced to return to Assyria. Twenty years later, Sennacherib was killed by two of his own sons.

Hezekiah also prayed to God at another crucial time in his life. Hezekiah became very sick. Isaiah warned the king that he would die. However, Hezekiah prayed to God and his life was spared for fifteen more years. Hezekiah died at the end of this fifteen year period. His son, Manasseh, began to reign as king and led Judah once again to idolatry.

## What You Should Learn

*1. The faithfulness of God.* God always is faithful to His word—He never breaks it. God promised that Sennacherib would not defeat Jerusalem. Both times God kept His promise. Today, God has made many promises to His children. If we will be faithful to God, He will fulfill His promises and give us many blessings (read 1 Cor. 1:9; 2 Cor. 1:20; Titus 1:2; 2 Pet. 3:9).

*2. The power of prayer.* When Hezekiah prayed to God and asked Him not to let Sennacherib defeat him, God listened. When Hezekiah prayed that his life be spared, God listened. When God's children pray today in faith, God listens (Jas. 5:16).

**The Taylor Prism contains Sennacherib's record of his invasion of Judah. The clay prism was found in Nineveh.**

## Review

### Short Answer

1. Look at the following names, and tell whether each was good or evil:

   a. Hezekiah _____

   b. Ahaz _____

   c. Sennacherib _____

d. Manasseh _____

e. Isaiah _____

f. Rabshakeh _____

2. When Hezekiah first began to reign, what did he do that pleased God? _____

3. Who was the prophet of God who comforted Hezekiah?_____

4. What nation was the enemy of Judah in this lesson? _____

5. What was the amount of tribute Hezekiah paid to Sennacherib?

_____

6. Why was Israel allowed to be defeated by the Assyrians, while Judah was not? _____

_____

7. What did Rabshakeh try to do? _____

_____

_____

8. What did Hezekiah do when Sennacherib told him to surrender?

_____

9. How did Sennacherib die?_____

_____

10. Who was the prophet of God who brought some bad news to Hezekiah? _____

11. What was the sign God showed Hezekiah that his life would be spared? _____

_____

## Matching

_____ 1. Nation which tried to help Judah     a. Ahaz

rebel against Assyria

_____ 2. The messenger of Hezekiah     b. 25 years

_____ 3.  The messenger of Sennacherib      c. Shalmaneser

_____ 4.  According to Isaiah's prophecy,    d. Sennacherib
          the nation which would later
          defeat Judah

_____ 5.  Father of Hezekiah                 e. Rabshakeh

_____ 6.  Son of Hezekiah                    f. Eliakim

_____ 7.  Amount of time Hezekiah's          g. Egypt
          life was spared

_____ 8.  The Assyrian king who tried        h. Babylon
          to capture Judah

_____ 9.  Age of Hezekiah when he            i. 15 years
          became king

_____ 10. The Assyrian king who did          j. Manasseh
          capture Israel

## True or False

_____ 1.  Hezekiah was able to save Judah because of his very
          strong army.

_____ 2.  Hezekiah was healed because of the power of God.

_____ 3.  A young man such as Hezekiah can be great in the sight
          of God.

_____ 4.  God kept all of His promises to Hezekiah.

_____ 5.  Sennacherib believed in God and worshipped Him.

Words to Know

*"Tribute"—money paid by one ruler or nation to another nation to denote subjugation*

# Josiah

**Lesson Objective:**
To emphasize that one can understand and know the will of God.

## MEMORY VERSE

*". . . Great is the wrath of the Lord that is aroused against us, because our fathers have not obeyed the words of this book, to do according to all that is written concerning us" (2 Kings 22:13).*

**READ:** 2 Kings 22:1-20; 23:1-30

**WHAT YOU WILL STUDY:** In this lesson, you will study the life of Josiah, who was king of Judah and very pleasing to God.

## The Story

In our last lesson, we studied about king Hezekiah. As you remember, Hezekiah was a very good king and was pleasing to God. His son, however, was a very wicked king. Manasseh led the people of God once again to commit idolatry. Manasseh was the grandfather of Josiah, the subject of this lesson. The father of Josiah was Amon. He also was a very wicked king. And so for fifty-seven years, Israel was again led into wickedness by these two kings.

Josiah was only eight years old when his father died. He was made king by the children of Israel in spite of his very young age! Josiah was not like his father and grandfather. Notice what the Bible says about him: "And he did what was right in the sight of the Lord, and walked in all the ways of his father David; he did not turn aside to the right hand or to the left" (2 Kings 22:2).

Because of the ways of Mannasseh and Amon, two things were true: the temple of God in Jerusalem had been defiled, and sacrifices were offered to idols throughout the land. This lesson tells how Josiah solved both of these problems.

The temple needed cleaning and repairing. Josiah sent Shaphan, a scribe, to arrange for carpenters and builders to do this job. As this work was being done, the high priest (Hilkiah) found "the book of the law." He brought it to Shaphan and Shaphan read the law to King Josiah. A prophetess named Huldah revealed that, because Israel had not obeyed this law for many

years, God was very angry. (Two other prophets lived during this time. They were Nahum and Jeremiah.) The words of Huldah saddened Josiah. He tore his clothes and cried. He then read the law to the people and they "made a covenant before the Lord." This meant that they agreed to obey Him. After this, Josiah and his people tore down places of idolatrous worship in many places: Kidron Brook, Geba, Beersheba, Topheth, Bethel, and other places. These idols had been built by many other kings (Ahaz, Manasseh, Amon, Solomon, and Jeroboam). But one king, Josiah, tore all of them down!

The Bible says of Josiah, "Now before him there was no king like him, who turned to the Lord with all his heart, with all his soul, and with all his might, according to all the Law of Moses; nor after him did any arise like him" (2 Kings 23:25). Josiah was a very great man in the sight of God.

## What You Should Learn

*1. The book of the law was found.* Can't you see how happy the high priest must have been when he found the law? It had been lost for many years, and yet he found it! Josiah was sad when he saw the law, but this was not because the law had been found. He was sad because the law had been lost so long and the people had forgotten it. Yes, it is always a joyful time when a person finds (or learns) the truth. Jesus told some parables about this. Read them in Matthew 13:44-46.

*2. The book of the law was read.* When Josiah heard the law, he ordered that it be read to the people. This was important. It is also important to read and study the Bible today. Read 2 Timothy 2:15. Are you reading the Bible?

*3. The book of the law was obeyed.* When the people heard the law, they decided to obey it. This is what God wanted them to do, and this is what He wants us to do today. When we hear the word of God and understand it, we should obey it.

The Assyrian god, Adad, god of Thunder, was a prominent deity worshipped in Josiah's day. The stela shows Adad standing on top of a bull.

## Review

### Matching

_____ 1. Grandfather of Josiah     a. Shaphan

_____ 2. Father of Josiah     b. Manasseh

_____ 3. Great-grandfather of Josiah     c. Judah

_____ 4. High priest     d. Hezekiah

_____ 5. Scribe and friend of Josiah     e. Amon

_____ 6. Nation Josiah ruled     f. Hilkiah

                                                          g. Israel

### Short Answer

1. How many years passed between the time of Hezekiah (our last lesson) and the time of Josiah (this lesson)?_____

2. Who was the mother of Josiah?_____

3. How old was Josiah when he became king? _____

4. What two big problems did Josiah solve while he was king?

    a. _____

    b. _____

5. What did the high priest find in the temple?_____

6. What prophetess revealed the wrath of God? _____

7. What did Josiah do when he heard the words of the prophetess?

    _____

8. Did the people promise to obey the law when it was read to them? _____

9. What idol is mentioned in 2 Kings 23?_____

10. What did Josiah do to these places of idolatry? _____

    _____

## Complete these lists:

1. Name five places where idolatry was torn down by Josiah:

   _____

   _____

2. Name five kings who had built these idols: _____

   _____

   _____

3. Name the two prophets (not prophetesses) who lived during this
   time. _____

## Fill in the Blanks

1. ". . . For great is the _____ of the Lord that is
   _____ against us, because our fathers have not
   _____ the words of this book, to do according
   to _____ that is written concerning us" (2 Kings 22:13).

2. "And he did what was _____ in the sight of the
   Lord, and walked in all the ways of his father David; he did not
   turn aside to the _____ hand or to the _____ " (2
   Kings 22:2).

3. "Now before him there was no king like him, who _____
   to the Lord with all his _____, with all his
   _____, and with all his _____, according to
   all the _____ of _____ . . ." (2 Kings 23:25).

# The Last Days of Judah

**READ:** 2 Kings 23:30-37; 2 Kings 24:1-16

**WHAT YOU WILL STUDY:** In this lesson, you will see how and why the kingdom of Judah was conquered by the kingdom of Babylon.

## The Story

In our last lesson, we studied about king Josiah. After he had been king for many years, Josiah met Pharaoh-necho (king of Egypt) in a battle. The king of Egypt killed Josiah at Megiddo.

After Josiah's body was buried, the people of Judah anointed Jehoahaz as king. Jehoahaz was the son of Josiah, but he certainly did not live like his father! Pharaoh-necho put Jehoahaz in prison after he had ruled for only three months. At the same time, the Egyptian ruler forced the people of Judah to pay a tribute tax. Jehoahaz was taken to Egypt, where he died. In his place, another son of Josiah was appointed king. His name was Eliakim, but Pharaoh-necho changed his name to Jehoiakim. Jehoiakim was also a very wicked man. For eight years, he paid tax to Egypt.

After this, however, king Nebuchadnezzar of Babylon made Jehoiakim serve him. The king of Judah served Nebuchadnezzar for three years, but then rebelled. When he did this, God caused his enemies to march against Judah and take the king into captivity. Daniel and his three friends, Shadrach, Meshach, and Abednego, were also taken captive at that time.

Jehoiachin (the son of Jehoiakim) was then appointed king. After a very short reign, Jehoiachin, his family, and the important people of Jerusalem were captured by Nebuchadnezzar, the king of Babylon. Nebuchadnezzar also took many treasures from the temple.

All during this time, God's prophet Jeremiah was begging the people of Judah to return to God. His whole message to the people is summed up in one verse: "'Return, you backsliding children, And I will heal your backslidings.' 'Indeed we do come to You, For You are the Lord our God'" (Jer. 3:22). Instead of listening to Jeremiah,

## Lesson Objective:
To stress that God will punish the disobedient

## MEMORY VERSE

"And he did evil in the sight of the Lord, according to all that his father had done" (2 Kings 24:9).

they rejected him and refused to repent. For example, at one time Jeremiah thought it would be good to have the messages from God written down—this might make a bigger impression upon the people. Therefore, Jeremiah dictated the word of God to Baruch, who wrote it down. Baruch read the scrolls in the temple, and some of the princes became interested. However, when king Jehoiakim heard about this, he had the scroll destroyed. More than once Jeremiah was thrown into prison, beaten, and almost killed. Because he was persecuted so much, Jeremiah found it difficult at times to preach the word of God. He grew very discouraged—but in spite of this, he remained faithful to God. He continued to tell the people that they would soon become captives of Babylon.

## What You Should Learn

*1. God still wanted His people to repent.* Isn't it amazing how longsuffering God was with His people? They had rejected Him again and again. They had worshipped idol gods. They had cursed His name. They had killed His messengers, the prophets. And yet, God still wanted His people to be righteous and to be saved from the destruction of an enemy army. Jesus told the Jews this very thing in His day. "O Jerusalem, Jerusalem, the one who kills the prophets and stones those who are sent to her! How often I wanted to gather your children together, as a hen gathers her chicks under her wings, but you were not willing!" (Matt. 23:37).

God is still longsuffering with the people of the world. Paul said in Romans 9:22-23, "What if God, wanting to show His wrath and to make His power known, endured with much longsuffering the vessels of wrath prepared for destruction, and that He might make known the riches of His glory on the vessels of mercy, which He had prepared beforehand for glory." God showed His longsuffering with man when He sent His son Jesus to this world: "whom God set forth as a propitiation by His blood, through faith, to demonstrate His righteousness, because in His forbearance God had passed over the sins that were previously committed" (Rom. 3:25). God is showing His longsuffering today by giving all people an opportunity to obey the gospel before He sends Jesus to judge the world: "The

Lord is not slack concerning His promise, as some count slackness, but is longsuffering toward us, not willing that any should perish but that all should come to repentance" (2 Pet. 3:9). The Bible teaches that we despise the longsuffering of God when we refuse to repent. Paul said, "Or do you despise the riches of His goodness, forbearance, and longsuffering, not knowing that the goodness of God leads you to repentance?" (Rom. 2:4).

*2. The people rejected Jeremiah.* Just as they had rejected all the other prophets, the people rejected Jeremiah. When Jesus came, many Jews rejected Him. Even today many people reject God by rejecting His word. Jesus said: "He who rejects Me, and

**The tel at Megiddo. The valley at Megiddo was a famous Hebrew battlefield like Shiloh or Gettysburg in the United States. Josiah was killed at Megiddo.**

does not receive My words, has that which judges him—the word that I have spoken will judge him in the last day" (John 12:48).

*3. Jeremiah continued to speak.* One of the saddest men in the Bible was Jeremiah. One of the most discouraged men in the Bible was Jeremiah. He tried to preach the word of God—and yet, the people rejected him every time. Still, Jeremiah continued to preach and to live righteously. We should do the same thing today. As we work and play with our friends, we should tell them about Jesus. Some of them might laugh at us. Others might talk about us. However, we should be like Jeremiah and continue to tell about Jesus. Christ Himself said, "If the world hates you, you know that it hated Me before it hated you. . . . Remember the word that I said to you, 'A servant is not greater than his master.' If they persecuted Me, they will also persecute you. If they kept My word, they will keep yours also" (John 15:18, 20).

## Review

### Short Answer

1. Did the sons of Josiah follow in their father's footsteps? _____

2. How long did Jehoahaz reign as king? _____

3. What did Egypt force the people of Judah to do? _____

    _____

    _____

4. What nation besides Egypt caused trouble for Judah? _____

5. Name some things that Nebuchadnezzar took from Judah when he invaded it. _____

6. List some good qualities of Jeremiah. _____

    _____

    _____

7. What was Jeremiah's message to the people of Jerusalem?

    _____

    _____

8.  How did the people of Judah receive Jeremiah's teaching? ___

_____

9.  Was God very longsuffering with the people of Judah?_____

10. Did God cause the nation of Judah to fall? _____Why? ____

_____

## Identify the Following

1.  Name the king who killed Josiah._____

2.  Name the place where Josiah was killed. _____

3.  Name the two kings of Judah who were the sons of Josiah. ___

_____

4.  Name the king of Judah who was the grandson of Josiah. ____

5.  Name the ruler of Babylon. _____

6. Name the prophet that was taken into Babylon by their king.

_____

7.  Name the three friends this prophet had._____

_____

8.  Name the prophet who preached to Judah._____

9.  Name the man who wrote Jeremiah's messages on scrolls.

_____

10. Name the king who had the scroll destroyed. _____

Words to Know

"Longsuffering"—love and patient endurance of injuries, insults, and troubles

# God Destroys His Holy City

**READ:** 2 Kings 24:17-20; 25:1-21; 2 Chronicles 36:10-21

**WHAT YOU WILL STUDY:** In this lesson, you will read about how God destroyed Jerusalem.

## The Story

We have been studying how the people of God went into captivity. First, the people of Israel (the northern kingdom) were defeated by the Assyrians in 722 BC. Then, the people of Judah (the southern kingdom) were defeated by the Babylonians in 606 BC. However, one "stronghold" of Judah remained—the city of Jerusalem. Now we are about to study how Jerusalem, God's "holy city," was destroyed by Babylon. Remember this throughout our study: All of this captivity and suffering came upon Israel and Judah because they turned away from God.

The prophets Jeremiah and Ezekiel were still preaching at this time. Jeremiah worked in Jerusalem while Ezekiel prophesied in Babylon. Jeremiah saw that the people would not repent; so, he tried to convince the people to surrender to Babylon. In Jeremiah 27:8, he said, "'And it shall be, that the nation and kingdom which will not serve Nebuchadnezzar the king of Babylon, and which will not put its neck under the yoke of the king of Babylon, that nation I will punish,' says the Lord, 'with the sword, the famine, and the pestilence, until I have consumed them by his hand.'" After Zedekiah became king of Judah, Jeremiah was accused of treason and put into prison. However, he was freed when an Ethiopian named Ebed-melech asked king Zedekiah to release him. While all of this was happening to Jeremiah, the prophet Ezekiel continued to tell the people that they would be conquered by Babylon. In Ezekiel 4-7, the prophet tells how terrible that day was to be for Jerusalem.

Sure enough, the words of Jeremiah and Ezekiel came true. The destruction of Jerusalem actually came in three different stages.

First, the Babylonians invaded Jerusalem during the reign of Jehoiakim. At that time, they captured Daniel (606 BC). We studied this in our last lesson.

**Lesson Objective:**
To emphasize God's justice in punishing sin.

## MEMORY VERSE

*"But they mocked the messengers of God, despised His words, and scoffed at His prophets, until the wrath of the Lord arose against His people, till there was no remedy"* (2 Chronicles 36:16).

**This small clay tablet contains a record of Babylonian history. It tells of the capture of Jerusalem, and of the removal of Jehoiachin to Babylon.**

Second, the Babylonians invaded Jerusalem during the short reign of Jehoiachin (597 BC). This time, they stole some treasures that were in the temple, captured king Jehoiachin, and took away many important people, including Ezekiel, back to Babylon. We also studied this in last week's lesson.

Third, the Babylonians invaded Jerusalem during the reign of Zedekiah. Nebuchadnezzar had put Zedekiah on the throne in Jerusalem. After a few years, however, Zedekiah rebelled against Nebuchadnezzar and Babylon. The king of Babylon finally lost patience with Jerusalem. He captured King Zedekiah. When he was brought before Nebuchadnezzar, his own sons were killed before his eyes. Then they "put out the eyes of Zedekiah." After this, Nebuchadnezzar sent Nebuzaradan, the "captain of the guard," to Jerusalem. When Nebuchadnezzar came to Jerusalem, he utterly destroyed the city. He set fire to the king's palace and to all the other houses in the city. He destroyed the beautiful temple that Solomon had built. He also took all except the very poor people out of Jerusalem. This happened in 586 BC. You have now seen how the once great Israelites became captives in foreign lands.

## What You Should Learn

*1. The prophecies of God came true.* In the last lesson, we studied the prophet Jeremiah. At that time, we saw that Jeremiah had predicted the fall of Judah and Jerusalem. The people did not believe him. They ridiculed his warnings and they denied his predictions. However, Jeremiah's prophecies came true. Jeremiah's prophecies came true because God always keeps His word. God still keeps His word today. He has made many promises to Christians. Faithful Christians know that He will keep His word. This is taught many times in the New Testament. In 1 Corinthians 1:9 and 1 Corinthians 10:13, Paul said, "God is faithful." In 2 Corinthians 1:20 Paul said, "For all the promises of God in Him are Yes, and in Him Amen" and Peter wrote, "The Lord is not slack concerning His promise, as some count slackness" (2 Pet. 3:9).

**2. God's longsuffering ended.** God was longsuffering with the people for many years. He gave them many opportunities to make their lives righteous. But when they rejected Him, God's longsuffering ended. God explained this in Proverbs 1:24-27: "Because I have called and you refused, I have stretched out my hand and no one regarded, Because you disdained all my counsel, And would have none of my rebuke, I also will laugh at your calamity; I will mock when your terror comes, When your terror comes like a storm, And your destruction comes like a whirlwind, When distress and anguish come upon you." Many people today are like the people of Jerusalem. God is giving them time to obey the gospel, but they refuse. One day, however, God's longsuffering will end. Christ will come and judge the world. Those who have not obeyed will be lost. Jesus explained this in Matthew 24:48-51: "But if that evil servant says in his heart, 'My master is delaying his coming,' and begins to beat his fellow servants, and to eat and drink with the drunkards, the master of that servant will come on a day when he is not looking for him and at an hour that he is not aware of, and will cut him in two and appoint him his portion with the hypocrites. There shall be weeping and gnashing of teeth."

The city of Jerusalem as it presently exists. The ancient city was destroyed by the Babylonians in 587 BC.

## Review

### Which Happened First? (Underline the correct answer.)

1. Capture of Israel           or      Capture of Judah

2. God punished Judah          or      Judah disobeyed God

3. Jeremiah asked Judah to     or      Jeremiah saw that Judah
   surrender to Babylon                would not repent

4. Jeremiah and Ezekiel        or      Jerusalem is destroyed
   prophesy about the                  by Babylon
   destruction of Jerusalem

5. Capture of Ezekiel          or      Capture of Daniel

### Who Did the Following?

1. Who defeated the nation of Israel? _____

2. Who defeated the nation of Judah? _____

3. Who prophesied that Jerusalem would be destroyed? _____
   _____ and _____

4. Who asked the king to free Jeremiah from prison? _____

5. Who was the king of Judah when the Babylonians invaded Jerusalem for the first time? _____

6. Who was the king of Judah when the Babylonians invaded Jerusalem for the second time? _____

7. Who was the king of Judah when the Babylonians destroyed
   Jerusalem?_____

8. Who was the king of Babylon that invaded Judah? _____

9. Who was the "captain of the guard" in the Babylonian army that
   destroyed Jerusalem? _____

### Tell what happened to the following when Jerusalem was destroyed:

1. Pillars of brass in temple _____

2. House of the Lord (temple) itself _____

3. King's house_____

4. Walls of Jerusalem_____

5. Utensils of gold and silver in temple_____

## Short Answer

1. How many years passed from the time when Israel was defeated by Assyria to the time when Jerusalem was burned by Babylon?

   _____

2. Why was Jeremiah put into prison? _____

3. What prompted Nebuchadnezzar to have Jerusalem destroyed?

   _____

   _____

4. What was done to the sons of Zedekiah? _____

   _____

5. What was done to Zedekiah himself? _____

# Seventy Years in Babylon

**READ:** 2 Kings 25:22-30; Psalm 137:1-9

**Lesson Objective:**
To emphasize God's promise to establish the church, to give hope to the captives.

**WHAT YOU WILL STUDY:** In this lesson you will see how the Jews were punished in Babylonian captivity. You will also study some events in the life of Daniel.

## The Story

In our last lesson, we saw that Nebuzaradan (who was captain of the guard) took many of the people of Jerusalem as prisoners into Babylon. However, the very poor Jews were allowed to stay in Judah to tend the gardens and vineyards of that land. Nebuchadnezzar appointed Gedaliah as governor over these poor people. Gedaliah tried to persuade these people to serve Babylon. It was not long, though, before a Jew named Ishmael killed Gedaliah. The rest of the Jews in Judah were afraid that Nebuchadnezzar would avenge the death of Gedaliah. Because of their fear, some of these poor Jews fled to Egypt.

When some of the Jews were taken to Babylon, Jeremiah prophesied that the captivity would last for seventy years. He said, "'And this whole land shall be a desolation and an astonishment, and these nations shall serve the king of Babylon seventy years. Then it will come to pass, when seventy years are completed, that I will punish the king of Babylon and that nation, the land of the Chaldeans, for their iniquity,' says the Lord; 'and I will make it a perpetual desolation'" (Jer. 25:11-12). This proved to be true. For seventy years the Jews had to live in a strange land away from home. For seventy years the Jews were so sad that they could not sing their songs or play their harps. For seventy years the Jews had to serve the Babylonians as common slaves. Life was so bad for the Jews during this time that they hated the Babylonians very much. They dreamed of the past when they were happy in Jerusalem serving God. They looked forward to the time when God would let them return to Jerusalem. The seventy years lasted from 606 BC, when the first group was taken to captivity, to 536 BC, when the first group returned.

## MEMORY VERSE

*"By the rivers of Babylon, There we sat down, yea, we wept When we remembered Zion" (Psalms 137:1).*

During this time, however, there were some Jews who were treated well by Nebuchadnezzar. One of these was Daniel.

Even as a young man, Daniel put his trust in God. As a result of this, God cared for him. When Daniel was first brought to Babylon, he and his three friends (Shadrach, Meshach, and Abednego) were offered some of the king's wine and his delicacies. All four boys refused to drink his wine or eat his delicacies. God rewarded their faithfulness by making them ten times wiser than all the others in the kingdom.

Nebuchadnezzar had a very strange dream one night. When he awoke the next morning, he forgot exactly what the dream was. The dream still troubled him, though, and so he sent for his magicians to tell him the dream. Of course, they didn't know what the king had dreamed. Nebuchadnezzar threatened to put to death his wise men, unless they would tell him his dream and its meaning. Daniel offered to interpret the dream for the Babylonian king. Nebuchadnezzar called in Daniel. Through the guidance of God, Daniel told the mighty king his dream and the meaning of it.

# Nebuchadnezzar's Dream
## Daniel 2:1-49

Head of Gold

Chest & Arms of Silver

Belly & Thighs of Bronze

Legs of Iron

Feet of Iron & Clay

**Four Kingdoms**

**Babylonian**
625-536 B.C.

**Medo-Persian**
536-330 B.C.

**Greco-Macedonian**
330-166 B.C.

**Roman**
63 B.C.-455 A.D.

In his dream, Nebuchadnezzar had seen a great image. It was very bright, but it looked very terrible. The head of the image was made out of gold. The arms and breast were made out of silver. The stomach and thighs were made from brass. The legs were composed of iron, and the feet were made from iron and clay. Then, without hands, a stone was cut out of the top of a mountain, and it rolled down the mountain, hit the image, and broke the image into many pieces. The stone became a great mountain, and it filled the whole earth.

**The beautiful Ishtar Gate from Nebuchadnezzar's palace in Babylon has been restored in the Pergamum Museum in Berlin, Germany. Daniel and his three friends must have seen and passed through this very gate.**

Daniel told the king the meaning of his dream. The head of gold on the image stood for the Babylonian kingdom. The other parts of the image represented other empires that would arise in the future. The legs and feet of the image represented the Roman empire. During the time of the Roman empire, Daniel prophesied that God would establish His kingdom. The kingdom of God was represented by the stone that was cut out of the mountain. It would be more powerful than any empires built by man, and it would spread throughout the earth. Daniel said, "And in the days of these kings shall the God of heaven set up a kingdom, which shall never be destroyed: and the kingdom shall not be left to other people, but it shall break in pieces

35

and consume all these kingdoms, and it shall stand for ever" (Dan. 2:44). As we today look at history, we see that God did establish His kingdom. It is the church. It was established in the days of the Roman kings. It still exists today, and those who obey God are members of it.

Years after Nebuchadnezzar had died, Nabonidus became king of Babylon. During his years as king, he left Babylon for an extended period of time and left Belshazzar in charge. Belshazzar called the important men of Babylon to attend a great feast. As everyone drank more and more wine, they became very drunk. They even drank wine from the gold and silver cups that had been taken from the temple in Jerusalem many years before. In the midst of all this sin, however, suddenly a hand mysteriously appeared. It was writing words on the wall. Horrified, the king called Daniel to him. Daniel told Belshazzar that the hand was the hand of God. The handwriting said, "This is the interpretation of each word. MENE: God has numbered your kingdom, and finished it; TEKEL: You have been weighed in the balances, and found wanting; PERES: Your kingdom has been divided, and given to the Medes and Persians" (Dan. 5:26-28). Cyrus invaded Babylon that very night. Darius the Mede received the kingdom. The Babylonian captivity was at an end!

## What You Should Learn

*1. God punishes evildoers.* When God's longsuffering with Judah ended, He punished all those that did not repent. And, as you read Psalm 137, you saw that the punishment was very great. The people of Judah suffered many hardships in Babylonian captivity but they had brought it upon themselves. When a man does evil, he

**36**

will be punished. This has always been true from the time of Adam to our present time. Jesus said in Matthew 16:27, "For the Son of Man will come in the glory of His Father with His angels, and then He will reward each according to his works." Many people think that our God of love will not punish anybody. Yes, God is showing his love now in giving everyone an opportunity to obey Him. But our God is also just, and He will show His justice in the judgment day: "But he that doeth wrong shall receive for the wrong which he hath done: and there is no respect of persons" (Col. 3:25).

*2. God cares for His own.* Daniel was treated well in Babylon because God cared for him. More than once, God saved Daniel from death. For example, when Daniel was in the lions' den, God stopped the mouths of the lions so that Daniel's life was saved. God saved the lives of Daniel's three friends, Shadrach, Meshach, and

**Cyrus and Darius were rulers of the Persian empire. Remains of its capital are displayed in this sunset photo at Susa.**

Abednego, when they were put into the fiery furnace. God cares for His children today. Christians have many good things that other people don't have. Some of these spiritual blessings are joy, peace, redemption, and many others. Paul spoke much about this. He said in 1 Corinthians 3:21-23, "Therefore let no one boast in men. For all things are yours: whether Paul or Apollos or Cephas, or the world or life or death, or things present or things to come—all are yours. And you are Christ's, and Christ is God's." He also said, "For all things are for your sakes, that grace, having spread through the many, may cause thanksgiving to abound to the glory of God" (2 Cor. 4:15).

*3. Revelling is a sin.* When Belshazzar gave his evil feast, he was committing the sin of revelling. Such things as drinking, dancing, cursing, and immoral behavior usually are a part of revelling. God was displeased because Belshazzar committed this sin. He will be displeased with us if we commit this sin today. In Galatians 5:21, Paul said that revelling is a "work of the flesh."

## Review

### Name the person:

1. Who was appointed as ruler over the poor people of Jerusalem?

   _____

2. Who was king of Babylon at that time? _____

3. Who killed the ruler of Jerusalem?_____

4. Who prophesied that the Babylonian captivity would last for seventy years?_____

5. Who was the prophet that was treated well by the Babylonian kings?_____

6. Who were the three friends of this prophet in his youth?_____

   _____

7. Who was the king of Babylon that gave a great feast and committed the sin of revelling? _____

8. Who was the man that became the ruler over Babylon? _____

   _____

## True or False

_____ 1. Some Jews were left in Jerusalem during the Babylonian captivity.

_____ 2. Although Jeremiah prophesied the Babylonian captivity would last seventy years, it only lasted fifty years.

_____ 3. All the Jews suffered in Babylon.

_____ 4. Of all the wise men that Nebuchadnezzar had, Daniel was the only one that could interpret dreams.

_____ 5. Belshazzar was a very righteous king.

**Nebuchadnezzar's Dream.** Supply the following information concerning the great dream you studied in this lesson:

1. Who dreamed it? _____

2. Who interpreted it?_____

3. Daniel was not able to tell Nebuchadnezzar what the dream was but was only able to tell what it means. (True or False?)_____

4. What were the following parts made of?

   Arms and breast_____

   Stomach and thighs _____

   Head_____

   Legs _____

   Feet _____

5. What did the following mean?

   Head of the great image_____

   Legs and feet of the great image _____

   Stone cut out of the mountain _____

6. After the stone was cut out of the mountain, what did it do? ___

   _____

7. What did this mean? _____

8.  The kingdom of God exists today. (True of False?) _____

9.  The dream came true. (True or False?) _____

10. The kingdom of God is the church. (True or False?) _____

## Short Answer

1.  When Gedaliah was killed, what did the poor Jews living in Judah do? _____

2.  Give at least one example from Daniel's life to show that he was a courageous person. _____

3.  Why was Daniel treated so well in Babylon? _____

4.  Why was Daniel able to interpret dreams? _____

5.  What great sin did Belshazzar commit?_____

6.  What nation defeated Babylon?_____

# The Return to Jerusalem

**READ:** Ezra 1:1-8; 2:64-70

**WHAT YOU WILL STUDY:** This lesson will tell the story of how the Jews returned to their homeland from Babylonian captivity.

## The Story

After Babylon was conquered, the Jews were under the control of the Persians. The king who defeated Babylon was Darius, the Mede. Just as Nebuchadnezzar and Belshazzar had treated Daniel well, the new king also liked Daniel very much. In fact, Darius had so much respect for Daniel that he made the prophet of God one of the three presidents of his kingdom. The presidents were second only to the king in authority and Daniel was the king's favorite president. With the other two presidents, Daniel was given power over 120 princes, who looked after the details of the kingdom of Persia. Because the other two presidents and princes were jealous of Daniel's position in the kingdom, they tricked Darius into casting him into a den of lions. However, when king Darius saw that the lions did not harm Daniel, the king directed that the prophet of God be removed from the den of lions, that the jealous presidents and princes be thrown into the den, and that the whole kingdom of Persia praise the "God of Daniel."

When Darius died, king Cyrus became ruler of the Persian empire. The Bible reveals that one of the first things Cyrus did as king

## MEMORY VERSE

*"All the kingdoms of the earth the Lord God of heaven has given me" (Ezra 1:2).*

41

of Persia was to issue a "proclamation." This proclamation permitted the Jews to return to their homeland of Judah and rebuild the temple in Jerusalem. Ezra writes that "the Lord stirred up the spirit of Cyrus, king of Persia," to issue this proclamation. This means that God's providence, in some way, moved Cyrus to do what he did. This shows that God had not forgotten His people; in fact, He intended all along for the Jews to be in bondage for seventy years and then be freed. For example, Jeremiah had prophesied, "'And this whole land shall be a desolation and an astonishment, and these nations shall serve the king of Babylon seventy years. Then it will come to pass, when seventy years are completed, that I will punish the king of Babylon and that nation, the land of the Chaldeans, for their iniquity,' says the Lord; 'and I will make it a perpetual desolation'" (Jer. 25:11-12; see also, Jer. 29:10). Furthermore, God had said 200 years before the Persians conquered the Babylonians that Cyrus would be the ruler to free the Jews: "Who says of Cyrus, 'He is My shepherd, And he shall perform all My pleasure, Saying to Jerusalem, "You shall be built," And to the temple, "Your foundation shall be laid"'" (Isa. 44:28; see also Isa. 45:1,13). God had kept His promise again.

The Cyrus Cylinder, in the British Museum, records Cyrus's conquest of Babylon and his decision to allow temples to be rebuilt in the lands which had been conquered by Babylon, just as Ezra described.

When this proclamation was announced, it brought great joy to the hearts of the Jews because they could finally go back home! Psalm 126:1-3 gives a good idea of how happy the people were: "When the Lord brought back the captivity of Zion, We were like those who dream. Then our mouth was filled with laughter, And our tongue with singing. Then they said among the nations, 'The Lord has done great things for them.' The Lord has done great things for us, And we are glad." King Cyrus made a prince of Judah, named Sheshbazzar (sometimes called Zerubbabel), the leader of the people who were returning to Jerusalem. Cyrus also ordered his treasurer, Mithredath, to return to the Jews those things which Nebuchadnezzar had taken from the temple seventy years before.

This photograph shows ruins of Persian palaces at Persepolis. Daniel, Nehemiah, Esther, and Ezra lived during the days of the Persian Empire.

These were valuable because they were expensive and because they belonged to God. Ezra writes that the total number of Jews who returned to Judah was 42,360. Added to this great number was 7,337 servants. Two hundred singing men and women also made the journey. The journey began in 536 BC. When this great number of people arrived at Jerusalem, they did not forget God. Ezra says the "chief of the fathers" gave of what they had in order that the building of the temple might begin. We shall study this in our next lesson.

However, not all of the Jews went back home. Many Jews remained in Babylon and in the eastern portion of the Persian empire. The book of Esther in the Old Testament tells about some of the Jews who stayed in Persia. The story of Esther is fascinating. King Ahasuerus (485-465 BC, better known as Xerxes) was not pleased with his queen, Vashti, because she refused to attend a feast which the king had commanded. When the king selected another queen, he chose a Jewish woman named Esther (whose Hebrew name was Hadasseh). Esther was a very good woman, because she was raised by a godly man (who was her cousin) named Mordecai. Because he respected Jehovah, Mordecai refused to bow down before the king's chief minister, Haman. This made Haman very angry, and he plotted to kill all the Jews. At a banquet, Esther told King Ahasuerus about Haman's evil plot. The king then decreed that Haman be killed for planning such a terrible crime. The courage of Esther and Mordecai is one of the most thrilling stories in the Old Testament.

## What You Should Learn

**1. God cares for His children.** Many people have wondered why the lions did not kill Daniel when he was thrown into their den. Daniel himself gives the answer in Daniel 6:22, "My God sent His angel and shut the lions' mouths, so that they have not hurt me, because I was found innocent before Him; and also, O king, I have done no wrong before you." King Darius asked in amazement, "Daniel, Daniel, servant of the living God, has your God, whom you serve continually, been able to deliver you from the lions?" (Dan. 6:20). Yes, God was able to deliver Daniel, and God is able to deliver us today from evil and sin. This doesn't mean that God's children never suffer or that they are never sad. But it does mean that, in the end, God's children will be blessed and happy in heaven.

**2. The providence of God rules the world.** Most of you probably think that the president runs the United States. Most Persians probably thought the king ran their country. But the Bible teaches that God really rules the nations of the world. This is called "providence." The word "providence" simply refers to God's control over the world so that He provides for His people. It was God who allowed the Persians to defeat the Babylonians. And it was God who decreed that the Persians should release the Jews. God rules all.

**3. Sin never pays.** Haman was a very famous man in Persia. He was respected by many people, even the king. However, when Haman planned to murder all the Jews, this was his downfall. Haman hoped to hang Mor-

decai, so he built some gallows. But when the king learned what was happening, he punished Haman. What happened to the gallows Haman built? "So they hanged Haman on the gallows that he had prepared for Mordecai. Then was the king's wrath pacified" (Esth. 7:10). Sin never pays!

## Review

**Short Answer.** Tell what the following kings mentioned in this lesson did:

1. Darius _____

2. Cyrus _____

3. Nebuchadnezzar _____

4. Ahasuerus _____

## Matching

_____ 1. Became jealous of Daniel      a. Mordecai

_____ 2. Prophesied about Cyrus 200     b. God
years before he lived

_____ 3. Cyrus's treasurer      c. Zerubbabel

_____ 4. Ahasuerus's first queen      d. Presidents

_____ 5. King Darius's favorite president      e. Mithredath

_____ 6. Esther's cousin      f. Vashti

_____ 7. Cast Daniel into lions' den      g. Isaiah

_____ 8. Wanted to kill all the Jews      h. Haman

_____ 9. Leader of the returning Jews      i. Daniel

____ 10. He caused Cyrus to free the Jews      j. Darius

## Fill in the Blanks:

1. "All the _____ of the earth the _____ _____ of heaven has given me" (Ezra 1:2).

2. "Then it will come to pass, when _____ years are completed, that I will punish the king of _____" (Jer. 25:12).

3. "Who says of _____, 'He is My shepherd, And

he shall perform all My pleasure, Saying to _____, "You shall be built," And to the _____, "Your foundation shall be laid"'" (Isa. 44:28).

4. "Then our mouth was filled with _____, And our tongue with _____. Then they said among the nations, "The _____ has done great things for _____" (Psa. 126:2).

5. "So they hanged _____ on the gallows that he had prepared for _____" (Esth. 7:10).

## Supply the Missing Numbers

1. Number of presidents under Darius. _____

2. Number of princes under Daniel. _____

3. Number of years Jews were in Babylonian captivity. _____

4. Number of years before Cyrus that Isaiah prophesied. _____

5. Number of Jews who returned to Judah under Zerubbabel. ___

6. Number of servants who returned under Zerubbabel. _____

7. Number of singing men and women who returned under Zerubbabel. _____

8. Date when the return occurred. _____

Words to Know

*"Providence"—foresight that provides what is necessary for one's care*

# The Temple Rebuilt

**Lesson Objective:**
To show that God enabled His people to return to their land rebuild their temple.

## MEMORY VERSE

*"But the eye of their God was upon the elders of the Jews, so that they could not make them cease till a report could go to Darius" (Ezra 5:5).*

**READ:** Ezra 3:1-3, 9-13; 4:1-24; 5:1-5

**WHAT YOU WILL STUDY:** This lesson shows how the Jews began to rebuild the temple and the trouble that happened to them because of this.

## The Story

It surely was a great sight to see almost 50,000 people marching on foot back home! It must have taken a long time to make the journey, and it was certainly tiring to walk all those hundreds of miles. When they reached Jerusalem, the Jews were very happy to be back home. But what they saw was very sad in a way. Imagine the disappointment of the people as they saw only a few stones of what once was the royal palace and fine houses. However, the worst sight was the ruins of Solomon's once-beautiful temple. There must have been tears as the people looked at these ashes and then remembered how great and beautiful the city used to be. But, at least, thousands of Jews were back home in Palestine. The Jews who chose not to come back to Palestine, but rather to stay in foreign lands, came to be called "Jews of the Dispersion." The Jews in Palestine were sometimes called "Hebrews" to distinguish the Hebrew speaking Jews from the Greek speaking Jews.

Soon after they arrived, all the people came together at Jerusalem to offer a sacrifice. Joshua and Zerubbabel found the big rock where the Lord's altar had once stood. They proceeded to built an altar upon that base. Then, for the first time in many, many years, a sacrifice was made to the Lord upon that altar. This was the way the people showed God how thankful they were to be back home. Their home, once called Judah, began to be called Judea. These Jews in Palestine were called "Jews," in reference to where they lived just as the Samaritans were so named from where they lived (Samaria).

In the next year, the people began to rebuild the temple under the leadership of Zerubbabel, the prince, and Jeshua, the priest. The first thing that had to be done was to clear the ground so that the temple could be built. After ordering stone masons to do this, Zerubbabel sent some messengers to Tyre and Sidon to buy some cedar trees. These great cedar trees were floated to Joppa, and then carried from Joppa to Jerusalem. Soon the foundation of the temple was laid, and the people praised the Lord "For He is good, For His mercy endures forever toward Israel" (Ezra 3:11). Not all the people were singing, though. Some of the old men who had seen Solomon's temple began to cry. They knew that this new temple would not be as lovely as the old temple of Solomon.

It wasn't long before some enemies tried to stop the Jews from building the temple. There were people in Judea other than the Jews. Some of them were called Samaritans. When the Jews had been removed from their land many years before, the Assyrians had brought other people into the land of Judea. And it was the grandchildren and great-children of these people who tried to stop the Jews. They were afraid that, if the Jews built their temple, they would become powerful and kill all the Samaritans. So, one day, these Samaritans came to Zerubbabel and said, "they came to Zerubbabel and the heads of the fathers' houses, and said to them, 'Let us build with you, for we seek your God as you do'" (Ezra 4:2). But Zerubbabel knew they were lying, so he refused to let the Samaritans help.

This incident made the Jews and the Samaritans bitter enemies for hundreds of years after this. It's not surprising that the Samaritans tried to get the Persians to prevent the Jews from building the temple. Cyrus, king of Persia, liked the Jews and would have helped them, but he died. The Persian king Ahasuerus, did not treat the Jews so favorably as did Cyrus. Then Artaxerxes became the king of Persia. The Samaritans wrote him a letter and said, "Let it now be known to the king that, if this city is built and the walls completed, they will not pay tax, tribute, or custom, and the king's treasury will be diminished" (Ezra 4:13). Artaxerxes believed this letter, so he stopped the Jews from building the temple. No work was done on the unfinished temple for several years.

After several years, two prophets of God spoke to the people. One was Haggai, and he said, "Go up to the mountain, and bring wood, and build the house; and I will take pleasure in it, and I will be glorified, saith the Lord" (Hag. 2:8). The other prophet, Zechariah, spoke: "The hands of Zerubbabel have laid the foundation of this house; his hands shall also finish it" (Zech. 4:9). When the Jews heard these words, they started work again on the temple. A short time later, Darius became king of Persia.

The new temple was finally finished twenty-one years after Zerubbabel began work on it. The new temple was not as beautiful and impressive as the one which Solomon had built. And, there was no Ark of the Covenant, for this had been lost for many years. But at least the Jews could worship God again in the temple.

## What You Should Learn

*1. The people were thankful to God.* When the Jews reached their homeland, they were very happy. Yet, they did not forget God. They built an altar and offered a sacrifice to the Father in heaven. In doing this, they were showing God how thankful they were. Often, when people are happy, they forget about God. We must never forget to thank God for the good things we have. "In everything give thanks: for this is the will of God in Christ Jesus concerning you" (1 Thess. 5:18).

*2. The people finished the new temple.* To build the temple was a big job. It required much time, many men, and much material. Yet, the people were determined to do it. When their enemies stopped them, the people put their faith in God and finished the job. Nothing is too great for us to do if we will put our faith in God and do it. "And God is able to make all grace abound toward you, that you, always having all sufficiency in all things, may have an abundance for every good work" (2 Cor. 9:8).

## Review

### Name the Place

1. Land to which the Jews went back. _____

2. City where the altar was built. _____

3. Cities from where the cedar trees came: _____ and _____.

4. City to which the cedar trees were floated. _____

5. Land over which Darius ruled. _____

## Name the People

1. What the Jews in Palestine were called. _____

2. What the Jews in other countries were called. _____

    _____

3. What people brought other nationalities into Palestine. _____

## Name the Persons

1. Name the priest in this lesson. _____

2. Name the people who cleared the ground for the temple. _____

3. Name the people who cried as the temple began to be built. __

    _____

4. Name the two prophets of God in this lesson. _____

    _____

5. Name four Persian kings mentioned in this lesson. _____

    _____

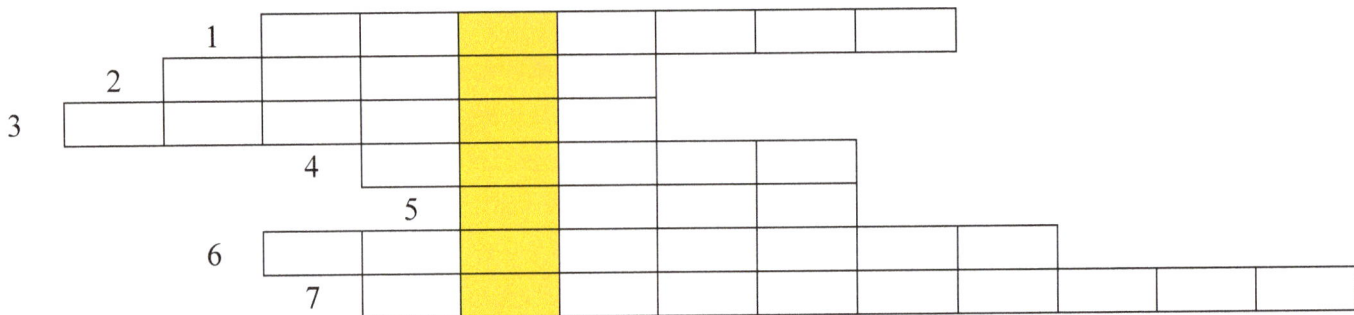

## Complete the Puzzle

Use the letters in the shaded spaces to spell a step in the plan of salvation. After hearing the gospel, we must __ __ __ __ __ __ __ it!

1. What the Jews in Palestine were called.

2. New name for Judah.

3. What the Jews rebuilt.

4. One of the cities which sent cedar trees

5. The book of the Bible in which you studied this lesson.

6. The ark which was missing the new temple ("Ark of the _____").

7. Leader of the Jews at this time.

# Ezra's Reforms

**Lesson Objective:**
To show that Ezra led a group of Jews back to Jerusalem.

**READ:** Ezra 8-10.

**WHAT YOU WILL STUDY:** This lesson discusses the work of Ezra in calling upon his people to obey Jehovah's will.

## The Story

When you read the lesson today you are taking a journey with men, women, and children who are going from Babylon to Jerusalem with Ezra. Several groups have already gone to Jerusalem and are settled there.

To begin the journey, Ezra appointed a place for them all to meet. It was at the river that ran to Ahava. This place was likely north of Babylon but no one knows exactly where it is located today.

### MEMORY VERSE

*"Then I proclaimed a fast there at the river of Ahava, that we might humble ourselves before our God, to seek from Him the right way for us and our little ones and all our possessions" (Ezra 8:21).*

When all the people first gathered and preparations were being made for the trip, Ezra discovered there were no Levites in the company. He sent a message to Iddo who was at Casiphia. The message requested he send servants who could minister at the house of God in Jerusalem. Over 200 came to go with them. Twelve of the chiefs among the priests were entrusted with much silver and gold for the temple. This had been given as a freewill offering to God.

When they began their journey, they had no soldiers to protect them. They trusted in God to keep them from the enemies along the way and He did. When they arrived in Jerusalem, they waited three days and, on the fourth day, the freewill offering was given at

the house of God and many burnt offerings were also made before God. The third thing they did was to deliver the commissions of the king of Persia to his lieutenants and the governors in that area.

## The Problem

Among the people who had gone to Jerusalem earlier, a serious problem had arisen. In Deuteronomy 7:3, God had commanded His people in the law given through Moses, "Nor shall you make marriages with them. You shall not give your daughter to their son, nor take their daughter for your son." God had forbidden the Israelites to intermarry with the people of the land of Canaan.

But, in the days of Ezra, the people had not listened to God and had intermarried. By the time Ezra had arrived, some of these Israelites with their foreign wives had children. And to make the problem worse, the princes and rulers among the people were among the main ones marrying foreign wives. With this as an example, it would only be an encouragement to the rest to feel this would be right for them also.

When Ezra heard this he said, "So when I heard this thing, I tore my garment and my robe, and plucked out some of the hair of my head and beard, and sat down astonished" (Ezra 9:3). Those who wanted to do the will of God came before him and he remained seated in this attitude of mourning until the evening sacrifice. He then turned his face to God and prayed in great sorrow and remorse for the people. Three things stand out in this prayer:

1. How unworthy man is before God.

2. God poured out His grace on His people anyway.

3. Ungrateful people go back into sin.

## The Reform

To please God, the people had to repent and put away their foreign wives. Shechaniah was the man who stated this in the presence of Ezra and the people. Of course, everybody who had come out of the captivity was not at Jerusalem at the time, so a decree was sent to all throughout the land telling the people to assemble

"And Ezra the scribe stood upon a pulpit of wood, . . . So they read in the book in the law of God distinctly, and gave the sense, and caused them to understand the reading" (Neh. 8:4, 8).

in Jerusalem in three days to hear God's word on this matter. Anybody refusing to come would lose his possessions and he would be separated from the congregation. When the people gathered this is what Ezra said: "Now therefore, make confession to the Lord God of your fathers, and do His will; separate yourselves from the peoples of the land, and from the pagan wives." The congregation answered, "Yes! As you have said, so we must do."

To see that this was done Ezra and certain ones who were leaders among the people were set up to judge the matter and the men came before them. This started the first day of the tenth month and was finished the first day of the first month.

This concluded the reform of Ezra as recorded in the book of Ezra.

## Have Fun And Learn by Doing.
Using the King James Version, read Ezra 8:1 and 21-36. Then mark whether the following statements are true or false.

_____ 1. When Ezra left Babylon, the king of Persia was Cyrus.

_____ 2. Preparations for the trip were made at the river of Ahava.

_____ 3. The men to whom the gold and silver were given were not priests.

_____ 4. The journey to Jerusalem took about four months (Ezra 7:8, 9).

_____ 5. One hundred ninety-seven animals were offered as burnt offerings to God at Jerusalem.

## Short Answer.
Read Ezra 9:5-5 and answer the following.

1. What had gone up unto the heavens? _____

2. What caused them to go into captivity? _____

3. What had been shewed from God to allow them to return?____

_____

4. What had God extended to them in the sight of the king of Persia?_____

5. Did Ezra say the people had been punished more than their iniquities deserved? _____

## Name the Person or Place

1. The Israelites left what country when they returned to their homeland? _____

2. Who led them during this journey?_____

3. To whom did Ezra send the message asking for Levites to accompany them on their journey? _____

4. On what river did they make preparation for the trip? _____

5. Who responded to Ezra's prayer saying the people had to put away their foreign wives?_____

## Fill in the Blanks

1. In chapter nine the princes told Ezra the people were doing the abominations of the nations around them. These nations were:

   _____ _____

   _____

   _____ _____

   _____

   _____ _____

   _____

2. The gold and silver were weighed out by Ezra to _____and _____ and ten of their brethren.

3. The house of the Lord was in _____.

# Nehemiah and the Walls of Jerusalem

**READ:** Nehemiah 1-6.

**WHAT YOU WILL STUDY:** This lesson will study the great work of Nehemiah, one of Israel's governors.

## Nehemiah in Shushan

Nehemiah was a close servant to the king, Artaxerxes, who ruled Persia. He served as his cupbearer. He also was a devout Israelite who wanted to hear that all was well with his people in Judea. Thirteen years before the time of our story, Ezra had taken a large number of Israelites back to Jerusalem, as we studied in the last lesson. In Ezra 7:8, we are told that Ezra returned in the seventh year of the king. In Nehemiah 1:1 we are reading about the twentieth year of the reign of the same king.

During these years all had not gone well in Judea. Hanani brought news to Nehemiah that the remnant was in great affliction and that the walls of Jerusalem were still broken down. With the permission of the king, Nehemiah returned to Jerusalem with the purpose of rebuilding these walls and setting up the gates of the city again.

## Two Problems

The king sent horsemen along with Nehemiah and also a letter to the governors requesting timber to aid in the rebuilding. When he arrived at Jerusalem he found two problems facing him.

1. Walls and Gates Completely Destroyed.

2. Enemies Opposing the Work of Rebuilding.

After Nehemiah had been in Jerusalem three days he went out by night to survey the damage around the walls and found it great in every direction. And, building a solid wall around city as large as Jerusalem had been was no small task.

In addition to that, Sanballat and Tobiah were strongly opposed to this. These men were not Israelites and, if the wall were rebuilt, it would strengthen the Jew's position and security in the land. They tried three things to defeat this work. One was the use of scorn and false accusation. They accused Nehemiah of rebuilding the walls so he could be king and rebel against the Persian king. He then attempted to raise military opposition against the project but through the wisdom and planning of Nehemiah that failed. They then tried to get Nehemiah to meet with them and talk over the situation. At least that is what they said, but Nehemiah knew they only wanted to kill or capture him and he refused to go. While all this opposition was going on Nehemiah had the people organized and the work progressing.

## The Walls Rebuilt

After Nehemiah surveyed the work to be done he organized the people into different working groups and put them to work on different parts of

the wall at the same time. This way it could be completed much more quickly.

But, while this was going on he planned for the protection of the people against Sanballat and Tobiah. This included part of the people working while part of the people watched. Also each man had his weapon with him at all times when he was working. But suppose the enemy found a weak spot in the wall and made an attack? What then? Nehemiah had a signal worked out that a warning would be given and all the people would rush to the section of the wall where the attack was made and fight together. The enemy was unable to stop the work.

## The Work Completed

According to Nehemiah 6:15 the walls were completed in fifty-two days. That may seem like a short time to complete this large

This view of the city of Jerusalem is taken from the Mount of Olives. One can see the walls around the city of Jerusalem which were built in 1538 by the Sultan of the Muslim Ottoman Empire, Suleiman the Magnificent.

task, but many people were involved and, according to the memory verse, the people had a mind to work. How long did it take to build the walls? _____

## Nehemiah's Reform

Remember the problem faced by Ezra? The people had married foreign wives. That is not the problem faced by Nehemiah. Chapter five shows the main problem of his day to be that of one Jew taking unfair advantage of another when times were difficult.

One verse shows Nehemiah's charge to the people in order to correct their wrongs. When you read this you will have some idea of what the Jews were doing to one another. The writer said, "Restore now to them, even this day, their lands, their vineyards, their olive groves, and their houses, also a hundredth of the money and the grain, the new wine and the oil, that you have charged them" (Neh. 5:11). God had forbidden them to charge interest or to take another's property. Yet they were taking advantage of one another in hard times and this was condemned and corrected.

## Have Fun and Learn by Doing.

**True or False.** Read Nehemiah 1 and answer True or False.

_____ 1. Nehemiah went to Jerusalem before Ezra did.

_____ 2. Chisleu brought Nehemiah news of the bad condition in Jerusalem.

_____ 3. Nehemiah did not pray to God about the problem.

_____ 4. Nehemiah did not say the Israelites had sinned.

_____ 5. Nehemiah was the king's cupbearer.

**Fill in the Blanks.** After Reading Chapter 3:1-6 answer the following questions:

1. _____ and his brethren built the sheep gate.

2. The fish gate was built by the sons of _____.

3. The nobles of the _____ did not put their necks to the work of the Lord.

4. The old gate was repaired by _____ and _____.

**Who Are They?** Read Nehemiah 2:10, 19, 20; 4:1-3, 7, 8; 6:1-8. Now write a brief description of the kind of men you think Sanballat and Tobiah were.

_____

_____

_____

_____

_____

**Places and People.** Define or identify the following:
1. Shushan (1:1). _____

2. Hanani (1:2) _____

3. Artaxerxes (2:1) _____

4. Asaph (2:8)_____

5. Sanballat _____

6. Ono (6:2) _____

# The Old Testament Closes

**READ:** Malachi (Read the entire book).

**WHAT YOU WILL STUDY:** This lesson will emphasize the problems addressed by the prophet Malachi.

## When Written

Because of internal evidence in the book, and conditions that are so much like those in Nehemiah, it is likely the book of Malachi was written during the same time. Most men, who have made a detailed study of the period of time and of the book itself, put the date of the book at 445 to 432 BC. The reason for these dates is that this is the period of time between Nehemiah's first visit to Jerusalem and his second visit. The only visit we studied in our last lesson was his first visit.

## Four Real Problems

*1. Polluted Offerings (1:6-8).* In the law of Moses God had specified the kind of sacrifices He wanted His people to offer Him. It was always one without blemish. Yet, at the time of Malachi the people were keeping the best for themselves and giving the lame, blind, and otherwise corrupted animals in sacrifice to God.

> **What about Today?**
> Is it not easy for us to do the same things today? If we have any time left over after we have done what we want we may read the Bible a little or go to a Bible class. Does the Lord come first with you?

*2. Insincere Worship (1:13, 14).* Some were saying, when they worshipped God, "what a weariness of it." They knew God required them to worship but they had rather be doing something else. They were just going through the form of worship but their hearts were not in it. When they made their offerings to God they complained about the drudgery of it. It was a tiresome thing. This is what was happening in 400 BC.

**Lesson Objective:**
To stress that one make a whole-hearted commitment to the Lord to be acceptable to Him.

## MEMORY VERSE

*"Behold, I will send you Elijah the prophet Before the coming of the great and dreadful day of the Lord. And he will turn The hearts of the fathers to the children, And the hearts of the children to their fathers, Lest I come and strike the earth with a curse" (Malachi 4:5-6).*

**3. *Divorce (2:14-16).*** In verse 16 the Lord shows His feelings about this practice which was common among His people. Men were putting away their wives and mistreating them. The Lord said, "He hates divorce." Divorce was granted by God under certain conditions in the Old Testament but His law did not mean anything to these people in Malachi's day. Have things changed much?

**4. *Robbing God (3:8-12).*** Under the Old Testament God required a tithe of all the people and numerous sacrifices in addition to this. In the fifth century before Christ the people were not giving as God commanded. When these people did not give as they were supposed to they were robbing God. These people likely would not go around robbing their neighbors and stealing from them. Yet, they were doing that very thing to God. God condemned the people for doing this to Him.

> **What about Today?**
>
> Anytime we refuse to give as God commands today we do the same to Him. Today we are to give as we purpose in our heart, as we prosper, cheerfully, and bountifully (2 Cor. 9:6-7; 1 Cor. 16:1-2). When we do not give this way, we do the same to God as the Israelites were doing in the days of Malachi. Now is the time for you to begin giving, whether you have little or much, as you follow God's instructions above.

These were some of the reforms that were needed in Malachi's day. They also are needed very much today in the lives of many.

## A Real Prophecy

Read Malachi 3:1 and. 4:5, 6. These verses speak of some time after the days of Malachi when Elijah would return. Now turn to these verses in the New Testament and see if you can figure who Malachi was referring to.

It is interesting that the New Testament begins (take Mark 1:2-5 for example) with the very verses that the Old Testament concludes with. Do these verses refer to Christ or John the Baptist? They all refer to the some one.

| **Who?** |
| --- |
| Mark 1:2 _____ |
| Matthew 11:1-15_____ |
| Luke 1:17 _____ |

## Have Fun and Learn By Doing

### Short Answer

1. When was Malachi likely written? _____

2. Who was guilty of these sins we discussed today—God's people or those who were not God's people? _____

   _____

3. What kind of animals were being offered to God? _____

_____

4. What prophet was supposed to return? _____

Did He? _____

5. Without looking back at your book and lesson list the four sins we discussed._____

_____

_____

_____

6. Of these four sins, which ones are men and women equally guilty of today?_____

_____

7. Discuss:

a. What can be done to keep our service to God from being a wearisome task? _____

_____

b. Do you believe you should wait until you are an adult before you start giving?_____

_____

c. Why does God hate divorce?_____

_____

_____

# The Division of the Kingdom

**A R A M (Syria)**

Sidon

Damascus

Mount Hermon

Tyre

**Kedesh** ✕

**DAN**
Dan

**MANASSEH**

Lake Huleh

*Geshur*

Accho

**NAPHTALI**

Hazor

**Golan** ✕

*Sea of Chinnereth*

*Bashan*

**ASHER**

**Phoenicia**

Mount Carmel

**ZEBULUN**

**ISSACHAR**
Jezreel

Yarmuk    River

Jabesh-Gilead

Ramoth-Gilead ✕

**THE GREAT SEA**

**MANASSEH**

**I S R A E L**

Mahanaim

Samaria ◎    Mount Ebal ▲

**GAD**

Mount Gerizim ▲ ✕ Shechem

Penuel

*Jabbok*

Joppa

Bethel   Shiloh

*River*

*Jordan River*

Jericho

*River*

Rabbath-Ammon

**EPHRAIM**

**DAN**

**BENJAMIN**

Gilgal

**Bezer** ✕

**AMMON**

Ekron

Jerusalem ◎

Medeba

Ashkelon

Bethlehem

**REUBEN**

Gaza

**JUDAH**

*Salt Sea*

Gerar    Ziklag

Hebron ✕

Arnon    River

Beer-Sheba

**MOAB**

**Philistia**

**N e g e v**

**SIMEON**

## Scale

N

| 0 | 10 | 20 | 30 | 40 |

Distance in Miles

⧄ Judah    ▭ Israel

**EDOM**

◎ Capital Cities    ✕ Cities of Refuge

64
64

www.ingramcontent.com/pod-product-compliance
Lightning Source LLC
Chambersburg PA
CBHW081251040426

42452CB00015B/2785